Beluga Whales

ABDO
Publishing Company

Big
Buddy BOOKS
Arctic Animals

by Julie Murray

VISIT US AT
www.abdopublishing.com

Published by ABDO Publishing Company, PO Box 398166, Minneapolis, Minnesota 55439.

Printed in the United States of America, North Mankato, Minnesota.
032013
092013

 PRINTED ON RECYCLED PAPER

Coordinating Series Editor: Rochelle Baltzer
Editor: Marcia Zappa
Contributing Editors: Megan M. Gunderson, Sarah Tieck
Graphic Design: Maria Hosley
Cover Photograph: *Shutterstock*: Miles Away Photography.
Interior Photographs/Illustrations: *Getty Images*: Visuals Unlimited, Inc./Louise Murray (p. 17), Flip Nicklin
    (pp. 7, 9, 23), Michael S. Nolan (p. 8); *Glow Images*: D.Fernandez & M.Peck/F1online (p. 11), imagebroker/
    Andrey Nekrasov (p. 13), Mark Newman (pp. 5, 19), Paul Souders (p. 11); *iStockphoto*: ©iStockphoto.com/alazor
    (p. 19), ©iStockphoto.com/nantela (p. 29); *Minden Pictures*: © Sue Flood/NPL (p. 21), © Flip Nicklin (p. 27);
    Photo Researchers, Inc.: Louise Murray (p. 9); *Shutterstock*: CampCrazy Photography (p. 25), J. Helgason
    (p. 15), Matthew Jacques (p. 4), Lykovata (p. 15), Christopher Wood (p. 4).

Library of Congress Cataloging-in-Publication Data

Murray, Julie, 1969-
  Beluga whales / Julie Murray.
    pages cm. -- (Arctic animals)
  ISBN 978-1-61783-798-2
  1. White whale--Juvenile literature. I. Title.
  QL737.C433M87 2014
  599.5'42--dc23
                    2012049641

Belugas are well built to live in different habitats. They can survive in near-freezing oceans or in warmer bodies of freshwater.

Belugas can live in shallow or deep water. They often stay near the surface.

Gulf of Alaska

BEAUFOR SEA

Welcome to the Arctic!

If you took a trip to where beluga whales live, you might find...

...islands.

The Arctic Ocean has many islands. Greenland is a large island that belongs to the country of Denmark. Canada has many islands in the Arctic. These include the Queen Elizabeth Islands and Baffin Island.

GREENLAND

(Kalaallit Nunaat)

GREENLAND SEA

SEA

nmark Strait

NORWEGIAN SEA

SEA OF
OKHOTSK

B
St

CHUKCHI SEA

IC OCEAN

North Pole

KARA
SEA

BARENTS
SEA

...Arctic sea ice.

The Arctic Ocean is covered by a thick sheet of ice. The sheet shrinks during summer and grows during winter. Beluga whales must stay south of the sea ice. If they don't, they can get trapped by it. This makes it hard for them to find air to breathe. And, it makes it easier for polar bears and humans to hunt them.

...narwhals.

These whales are the only other animals closely related to belugas. Narwhals have a long tooth that pokes through their upper lip. So, they are often called "the unicorns of the sea."

Take a Closer Look

Beluga whales have long, rounded bodies and short flippers. They have white skin. Unlike many related animals, belugas do not have fins on their backs.

A beluga's head has small eyes and a short, wide **beak**. The forehead has a large lump called a melon.

Uncovered!

Not having fins on their backs helps belugas survive in the Arctic. It allows them to swim right underneath ice while searching for breathing holes. And, it helps keep them warm because fins let heat escape.

Beluga whales belong to the toothed whales animal group. They have about 34 teeth.

During the winter, belugas may turn a yellowish color. Each summer, they shed their skin by rubbing on the ocean floor. Then, they are bright white again.

Belugas are one of the smallest types of whales. Adults are 10 to 20 feet (3 to 6 m) long. They weigh about 1,500 to 3,300 pounds (680 to 1,500 kg). Females are smaller than males.

Much of a beluga's large size comes from a thick layer of fat under its skin. This fat is called blubber. It can be up to six inches (15 cm) thick! Blubber helps trap heat inside the whale's body.

A beluga's belly often has thick folds of blubber.

Water World

Beluga whales are well built for life underwater. A beluga uses its tail to paddle while swimming. It uses its short, rounded flippers to change direction.

Belugas are generally slow swimmers. They swim about two to six miles (3 to 10 km) per hour.

Uncovered!
Belugas can dive deeper than 1,000 feet (300 m)!

A whale's tail has two parts called flukes. They move up and down together.

A beluga can change direction easily using its flippers. It can even swim backward!

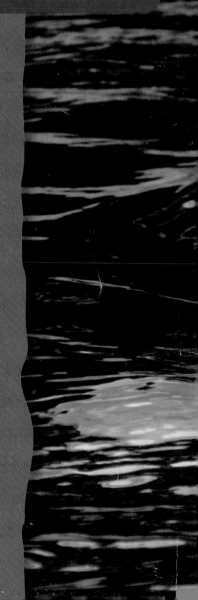

When belugas breathe out, they often shoot water into the air. This is called a blow. A beluga's blow is about 35 inches (90 cm) high.

Beluga whales breathe air through blowholes on the tops of their heads. So, they usually swim near the water's surface.

A beluga's blowhole is covered by a tight flap of skin. Just before the whale reaches the surface, it opens the flap and breathes out. At the surface, it breathes in quickly. Then, it closes the flap before going back underwater.

Uncovered!
A beluga whale can stay underwater for about 15 minutes.

Sensing with Sound

Uncovered!
Other animals, such as dolphins and bats, also use echolocation.

Beluga whales can see well underwater. But, they also sense in a special way called echolocation (eh-koh-loh-KAY-shuhn).

To do this, a beluga whale makes a clicking sound. The sound bounces off objects and returns to the whale. It tells the whale about its surroundings. This is useful for finding prey and breathing holes.

Echolocation tells a beluga about an object's size, shape, speed, and distance. It may even tell a whale about an object's insides.

Scientists believe belugas use their melons to echolocate. These bumps change shape when beluga whales make sounds.

Mealtime

Beluga whales are **carnivores**. They eat squid, shrimps, mussels, and worms. Most of these animals live on the ocean floor. Belugas use their mouths to suck them up. They spit jets of water to uncover food buried in sand or mud.

Beluga whales also eat many types of fish. These include cod, salmon, smelt, char, and herring. Belugas work together to hunt schools of fish. They herd them into shallow water, where they are easier to catch.

Uncovered!
Belugas often work in groups of five or more while hunting fish.

Belugas do not chew their food. They swallow it whole.

Social Life

Beluga whales are **social** animals. They live in groups called pods. A pod may have 2 to more than 25 whales. Most pods have about 10 members.

Belugas are loud! They make many sounds to share their feelings. These include clicks, grunts, clangs, whistles, and squeals. They also share their feelings by making faces and touching each other.

Uncovered!
Belugas are often called "sea canaries" because of the many loud noises they make. Their noises can even be heard through the bottom of a ship!

22

When belugas migrate, pods often join together. They may form groups of a few hundred to several thousands of whales!

23

Baby Belugas

Beluga whales are **mammals**. A female usually has one baby at a time. She gives birth every two to three years.

Baby whales are called calves. At birth, a calf is about five feet (1.5 m) long. It weighs about 120 to 175 pounds (54 to 80 kg).

Newborn belugas are dark gray or brown. Their skin changes color as they grow.

Uncovered!
Sometimes, a beluga calf rides on its mother's back while swimming.

A beluga calf can swim right after it's born. It stays close to its mother and drinks her milk. She teaches it how to catch food and **survive** in Arctic waters.

After about a year, beluga calves start eating food. They stop drinking milk after about two years. Calves are fully grown after about ten years.

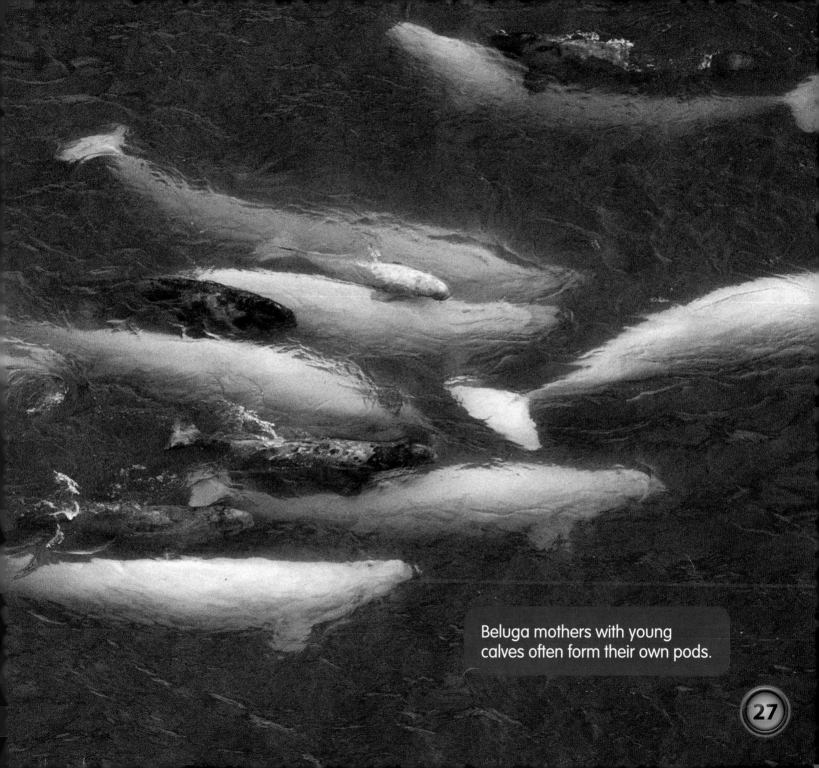

Beluga mothers with young calves often form their own pods.

Survivors

Life in the Arctic isn't easy for beluga whales. Long ago, people commonly hunted them for their blubber and meat. Today, **pollution** and businesses such as oil harm their **habitat**.

Still, these whales **survive**. Laws limit hunting them. And, people work to make sure they have large, clean places to live freely. Beluga whales help make the Arctic an amazing place.

Uncovered!
Belugas are near threatened. This means they are in a little danger of dying out.

In the wild, beluga whales live for 25 to 50 years.

Wow!
I'll bet you never knew...

...that beluga whale brains are missing the area used for smelling. So, scientists believe these whales can't smell.

...that unlike most whales, belugas have bendable necks. They can nod and turn their heads in all directions.

...that a beluga's flippers have bones for five fingers. But, the skin around them is connected. That makes it easier to swim.

...that the beluga whale's scientific name, *Delphinapterus leucas*, means "white dolphin without a fin."

Important Words

beak a hard mouthpart that sticks out.

carnivore (KAHR-nuh-vawr) an animal or a plant that eats meat.

continent one of Earth's seven main land areas.

habitat a place where a living thing is naturally found.

mammal a member of a group of living beings. Mammals make milk to feed their babies and usually have hair or fur on their skin.

migrate to move from one place to another to find food or have babies.

pollution human waste that dirties or harms air, water, or land.

region a large part of the world that is different from other parts.

social (SOH-shuhl) naturally living or growing in groups.

survive to continue to live or exist.

Web Sites

To learn more about beluga whales, visit ABDO Publishing Company online. Web sites about beluga whales are featured on our Book Links page. These links are routinely monitored and updated to provide the most current information available.

www.abdopublishing.com

Index